ROSE
of AUDACITY

The Courage to BLOOM

A 30 Day Journal and Guide for Courage and Confidence

*How to take back your power
and live an audacious life*

Virlynn Smith Randolph

ISBN: 978-0-578-63339-8

Copyright © 2019. Virlynn Smith Randolph. All rights reserved.

How to Use This Journal and Guide

Each day for the next 30 days you will receive a **ROSE**. What better way to start your day than receiving a **ROSE** of confidence and courage each morning!

Each of these **ROSES** have been carefully selected to express to you JUST how special you are. Make sure you use these **ROSES** (Affirmations) as a conversation with yourself about your greatness. Feel free to write them over and over, say them over and over, and remember them whenever you are tempted to tell yourself something OTHER than you have the RIGHT to Bloom.

Remember that your courage and confidence is just as much a result of what you tell yourself as what others have told you, so THIS is the chance to re-write the conversation about who you are.

YOU are a **ROSE**. WHY? Because I said so. And God did too!

Copyright © 2019. Virlynn Smith Randolph. All rights reserved.

The Courage to BLOOM Journal & Guide

Continuing to Bloom Resources

The 4 Agreements by Don Miquel Ruiz

As a Man Thinketh by James Allen

Battlefield of the Mind by Joyce Myers

Your Bible Written by God, Told by Man

The Rose of Audacity Book by Virlynn Smith Randolph

Copyright © 2019. Virlynn Smith Randolph. All rights reserved.

The Courage to BLOOM Journal & Guide

Day 1

I am special and the world needs me.

With so many people in the world, it is easy to get caught up with not feeling as if you make a difference. But remember, EVEN with so many people in the world, God took the time to make YOU different. That HAD to have been for a reason. Don't get caught up in what others are doing. Instead, take the opportunity to make a difference for someone every day. Even ONE life impacted is enough to make a difference.

Copyright © 2019. Virlynn Smith Randolph. All rights reserved.

The Courage to BLOOM Journal & Guide 🌹

Daily Reflections of a Rose

_____
_____
_____
_____
_____
_____
_____
_____
_____
_____
_____
_____
_____
_____
_____
_____
_____
_____
_____
_____
_____
_____
_____
_____
_____
_____
_____
_____

Copyright © 2019. Virlynn Smith Randolph. All rights reserved.

The Courage to BLOOM Journal & Guide

Day 2

Today I celebrate my small wins.

Sometimes we look at the success of others and wonder how they got there. Trust me, it was through a series of small, consistent steps. Some days your progress may be almost imperceptible. Almost. But as long as you know you are moving forward, that is enough to celebrate. LIFE is enough to celebrate.

Copyright © 2019. Virlynn Smith Randolph. All rights reserved.

The Courage to BLOOM Journal & Guide

Daily Reflections of a Rose

Copyright © 2019. Virlynn Smith Randolph. All rights reserved.

The Courage to BLOOM Journal & Guide 🌹

Day 3

Today I will be nice to ME.

It is amazing how often we get caught up pleasing others and fail the person that matters most... US.

Today, do something special for yourself. Treat yourself as you treat others. Say something NICE to you. Do something NICE for you. I am SURE you will appreciate it.

Copyright © 2019. Virlynn Smith Randolph. All rights reserved.

The Courage to BLOOM Journal & Guide

Daily Reflections of a Rose

_____
_____
_____
_____
_____
_____
_____
_____
_____
_____
_____
_____
_____
_____
_____
_____
_____
_____
_____
_____
_____
_____
_____
_____
_____
_____
_____

Copyright © 2019. Virlynn Smith Randolph. All rights reserved.

The Courage to BLOOM Journal & Guide

Day 4

It's OK to put myself first sometimes.

It's true that most of us live a life of sacrifice. We are Mom's first. Wives first. Daughters first. But today, and every now and then, don't forget to put yourself first. Think of life as a cup and make sure you are serving from your overflow and not from your lack. Honestly you can do MORE for others when you put yourself first.

Copyright © 2019. Virlynn Smith Randolph. All rights reserved.

The Courage to BLOOM Journal & Guide 🌹

Daily Reflections of a Rose

_____
_____
_____
_____
_____
_____
_____
_____
_____
_____
_____
_____
_____
_____
_____
_____
_____
_____
_____
_____
_____
_____
_____
_____
_____

Copyright © 2019. Virlynn Smith Randolph. All rights reserved.

The Courage to BLOOM Journal & Guide

Day 5

I deserve happiness and love.

Yes. I am tempted to leave that RIGHT there. God put you here to be happy and to be loved. Refuse anything but that. Do what makes you happy. Refuse anything that makes you unhappy. Expect to receive the same love you are putting out to others.

Copyright © 2019. Virlynn Smith Randolph. All rights reserved.

The Courage to BLOOM Journal & Guide 🌹

Daily Reflections of a Rose

_____
_____
_____
_____
_____
_____
_____
_____
_____
_____
_____
_____
_____
_____
_____
_____
_____
_____
_____
_____
_____
_____
_____
_____
_____
_____
_____

Copyright © 2019. Virlynn Smith Randolph. All rights reserved.

The Courage to BLOOM Journal & Guide 🌹

Day 6

I expect the kindness in return that I share with others.

Being kind is a deliberate act. We are KIND on purpose. As a kind person, it is OK to expect kindness in return. Refuse any situation that is not rooted in kindness. You have choices. When it is all said and done, if you don't accept what others give you that is not kindness, then it can't impact you.

Copyright © 2019. Virlynn Smith Randolph. All rights reserved.

The Courage to BLOOM Journal & Guide 🌹

Daily Reflections of a Rose

_____
_____
_____
_____
_____
_____
_____
_____
_____
_____
_____
_____
_____
_____
_____
_____
_____
_____
_____
_____
_____
_____
_____
_____
_____
_____
_____
_____
_____
_____

Copyright © 2019. Virlynn Smith Randolph. All rights reserved.

The Courage to BLOOM Journal & Guide

Day 7

I love myself and do my best to show it.

When was the last time you did something special for you? Said something nice to yourself? Told YOU that you LOVE YOU?!

Make today that day and, in fact, wake up DAILY telling yourself that you LOVE YOU. And don't just say it, show it.

The Courage to BLOOM Journal & Guide 🌹

Daily Reflections of a Rose

_____
_____
_____
_____
_____
_____
_____
_____
_____
_____
_____
_____
_____
_____
_____
_____
_____
_____
_____
_____
_____
_____
_____
_____
_____
_____

Copyright © 2019. Virlynn Smith Randolph. All rights reserved.

The Courage to BLOOM Journal & Guide

Day 8

My best is enough for those who love me.

There are things I am good at and things I am not so good. But for those that love you, your BEST is enough. If you are not a good cook and you make sandwiches, if someone loves you, it is enough. Give yourself credit for the things that you do well and don't overthink the things you don't do well. No one is good at everything and that is what makes us UNIQUE.

Copyright © 2019. Virlynn Smith Randolph. All rights reserved.

The Courage to BLOOM Journal & Guide

Daily Reflections of a Rose

_____
_____
_____
_____
_____
_____
_____
_____
_____
_____
_____
_____
_____
_____
_____
_____
_____
_____
_____
_____
_____
_____
_____
_____
_____
_____

Copyright © 2019. Virlynn Smith Randolph. All rights reserved.

The Courage to BLOOM Journal & Guide 🌹

Day 9

I am perfect just the way God made me.

While no one is perfect, we know that GOD was deliberate when He made us. He made us the way, He made us for HIS WILL, not ours. WE must NOT only accept our differences but also embrace them.

If they were enough for GOD, then they have to be enough for us.

The Courage to BLOOM Journal & Guide 🌹

Daily Reflections of a Rose

_____
_____
_____
_____
_____
_____
_____
_____
_____
_____
_____
_____
_____
_____
_____
_____
_____
_____
_____
_____
_____
_____
_____
_____
_____
_____

Copyright © 2019. Virlynn Smith Randolph. All rights reserved.

The Courage to BLOOM Journal & Guide 🌹

Day 10

I love my body. It is capable of doing amazing things.

No one has the same body type. While everyone has things they would like to change about their body, we can't forget the amazing things our body is capable of. How our eyes can see, and our ears can hear, and how our arms and legs make us mobile. Today, celebrate your body and all that it can do.

Copyright © 2019. Virlynn Smith Randolph. All rights reserved.

The Courage to BLOOM Journal & Guide 🌹

Daily Reflections of a Rose

_____
_____
_____
_____
_____
_____
_____
_____
_____
_____
_____
_____
_____
_____
_____
_____
_____
_____
_____
_____
_____
_____
_____
_____
_____
_____
_____
_____
_____
_____
_____
_____

The Courage to BLOOM Journal & Guide

Day 11

I am strong and will continue to become stronger.

Confidence is a muscle. Courage is a muscle. The more you move outside of your comfort zone, the more you will receive confidence and courage in exchange. Today look to do something different. Do the same thing the next day. Keep doing small things that change your life over time, and you will find it gets easier and easier.

Copyright © 2019. Virlynn Smith Randolph. All rights reserved.

The Courage to BLOOM Journal & Guide 🌹

Daily Reflections of a Rose

_____
_____
_____
_____
_____
_____
_____
_____
_____
_____
_____
_____
_____
_____
_____
_____
_____
_____
_____
_____
_____
_____
_____
_____

Copyright © 2019. Virlynn Smith Randolph. All rights reserved.

The Courage to BLOOM Journal & Guide

Day 12

I am grateful for today and will look for great things to happen for me.

It is easy to get caught up in 'why not me' mode. The fix to that is being grateful. Even on a bruised apple, it is not all bad.

Today, choose to cut off the bad parts and celebrate the rest of the apple. When we look for grateful, life finds a way of giving us more to be grateful for.

Copyright © 2019. Virlynn Smith Randolph. All rights reserved.

The Courage to BLOOM Journal & Guide

Daily Reflections of a Rose

_____
_____
_____
_____
_____
_____
_____
_____
_____
_____
_____
_____
_____
_____
_____
_____
_____
_____
_____
_____
_____
_____
_____
_____
_____

Copyright © 2019. Virlynn Smith Randolph. All rights reserved.

The Courage to BLOOM Journal & Guide 🌹

Day 13

I know I was created for a purpose. Today I celebrate my gifts.

Make a list of things you are good at. Make a list of things you are great at. Make a list of things that others compliment you on. EVERYONE is good at something. Celebrate those talents and spend your time growing your gifts. You will find that the more you celebrate your own gifts, others will too.

Copyright © 2019. Virlynn Smith Randolph. All rights reserved.

The Courage to BLOOM Journal & Guide 🌹

Daily Reflections of a Rose

_____
_____
_____
_____
_____
_____
_____
_____
_____
_____
_____
_____
_____
_____
_____
_____
_____
_____
_____
_____
_____
_____
_____
_____
_____
_____
_____
_____
_____
_____

Copyright © 2019. Virlynn Smith Randolph. All rights reserved.

The Courage to BLOOM Journal & Guide

Day 14

I am beautiful and worthy of beautiful things.

Just like all babies are beautiful to their mothers, we are all beautiful in the eyes of our Father. Beautiful things don't mean expensive things. Treat yourself to a single beautiful flower. Take the time to appreciate it and watch it bloom. Compare it to your own life and appreciate the beauty of how that ONE flower is different from all others... and you are too.

Copyright © 2019. Virlynn Smith Randolph. All rights reserved.

The Courage to BLOOM Journal & Guide

Daily Reflections of a Rose

Copyright © 2019. Virlynn Smith Randolph. All rights reserved.

The Courage to BLOOM Journal & Guide 🌹

Day 15

I live to be a positive influence to myself and others.

Our center of positivity must start with us. Just as Roses struggle to grow in rocky ground, people do too. As you increate your positivity, know that it is OK to remove yourself from situations, conversations, and people who are not a positive influence on you. Make sure that you approach others with positivity as well.

Copyright © 2019. Virlynn Smith Randolph. All rights reserved.

The Courage to BLOOM Journal & Guide

Daily Reflections of a Rose

_____
_____
_____
_____
_____
_____
_____
_____
_____
_____
_____
_____
_____
_____
_____
_____
_____
_____
_____
_____
_____
_____
_____
_____
_____
_____
_____

Copyright © 2019. Virlynn Smith Randolph. All rights reserved.

The Courage to BLOOM Journal & Guide

Half Point Check-in

Congratulations! You are half the way on your journey. How are you feeling so far? Have others noticed that you have started to shift? Have you noticed it? Are you being consistent in your daily affirmations?

If you are feeling good about yourself so far on this journey, keep going there is more to come.

If you haven't been consistent it's OK, Rome wasn't built in a day and confidence is not either.

Applaud yourself for getting this far EVEN if it took you time to get here. Now keep going!

Copyright © 2019. Virlynn Smith Randolph. All rights reserved.

The Courage to BLOOM Journal & Guide 🌹

Daily Reflections of a Rose

_____
_____
_____
_____
_____
_____
_____
_____
_____
_____
_____
_____
_____
_____
_____
_____
_____
_____
_____
_____
_____
_____
_____
_____
_____
_____

Copyright © 2019. Virlynn Smith Randolph. All rights reserved.

The Courage to BLOOM Journal & Guide 🌹

Day 16

Today I take responsibility for my own happiness.

Too often we expect others to make us happy. The truth is most people can't even make themselves happy, much less you. Today, take back control of YOUR happiness by doing things that make you happy. Granted, we won't LOVE everything we do each day, however, it is up to you to BE HAPPY even while doing things you may not necessarily enjoy. Happiness is YOUR choice and YOUR right.

Copyright © 2019. Virlynn Smith Randolph. All rights reserved.

The Courage to BLOOM Journal & Guide

Daily Reflections of a Rose

_____
_____
_____
_____
_____
_____
_____
_____
_____
_____
_____
_____
_____
_____
_____
_____
_____
_____
_____
_____
_____
_____
_____
_____

Copyright © 2019. Virlynn Smith Randolph. All rights reserved.

The Courage to BLOOM Journal & Guide

Day 17

I choose to surround myself by beautiful people and beautiful things.

By beautiful, I don't mean how people look on the outside or material things. I mean the spirit of beautiful. Sunrises and Sunsets are beautiful.

When you CHOOSE who and how you spend your time, you will be surprised by how much beauty you feel on the inside.

Copyright © 2019. Virlynn Smith Randolph. All rights reserved.

The Courage to BLOOM Journal & Guide 🌹

Daily Reflections of a Rose

_____
_____
_____
_____
_____
_____
_____
_____
_____
_____
_____
_____
_____
_____
_____
_____
_____
_____
_____
_____
_____
_____
_____
_____
_____
_____
_____
_____

The Courage to BLOOM Journal & Guide 🌹

Day 18

I can accomplish any goal I set my mind to.

Just like increasing your courage and confidence is a muscle, accomplishing your goals are too. Think back to a time where you accomplished something that was hard. At the time you may have thought you couldn't do it. But some kind of way you pulled it off. If you can pull off that one thing, you can do more, if you let yourself.

Copyright © 2019. Virlynn Smith Randolph. All rights reserved.

The Courage to BLOOM Journal & Guide 🌹

Daily Reflections of a Rose

_____
_____
_____
_____
_____
_____
_____
_____
_____
_____
_____
_____
_____
_____
_____
_____
_____
_____
_____
_____
_____
_____
_____
_____
_____
_____
_____

Copyright © 2019. Virlynn Smith Randolph. All rights reserved.

The Courage to BLOOM Journal & Guide 🌹

Day 19

I ask the Lord for what and He will honor it because I am His child.

I am amazed by how many people are afraid to ask for more. Asking for more is not being ungrateful. Asking for more is about understanding who your Father is and that He delights in giving you the desires of your heart.

Copyright © 2019. Virlynn Smith Randolph. All rights reserved.

The Courage to BLOOM Journal & Guide

Daily Reflections of a Rose

_____
_____
_____
_____
_____
_____
_____
_____
_____
_____
_____
_____
_____
_____
_____
_____
_____
_____
_____
_____
_____
_____
_____
_____
_____
_____

The Courage to BLOOM Journal & Guide 🌹

Day 20

Even during hardships I know that I am blessed and that change will come.

Life is not only about the ups, but about the downs as well. But know that change will come and that even in the hardships, there are some who are not as blessed as you.

Hang in there. All situations change over time. Don't let that be a deterrent to living a great life.

The Courage to BLOOM Journal & Guide 🌹

Daily Reflections of a Rose

_____
_____
_____
_____
_____
_____
_____
_____
_____
_____
_____
_____
_____
_____
_____
_____
_____
_____
_____
_____
_____
_____
_____
_____
_____
_____

Copyright © 2019. Virlynn Smith Randolph. All rights reserved.

The Courage to BLOOM Journal & Guide

Day 21

I am grateful for each small step I take towards my future.

There is a Chines philosopher that says the journey of a thousand miles starts with one step. The key is to keep taking those steps, while ever so small to where you want to be.

What is something you want to change and when will you point your toes in that direction?

Copyright © 2019. Virlynn Smith Randolph. All rights reserved.

The Courage to BLOOM Journal & Guide 🌹

Daily Reflections of a Rose

_____
_____
_____
_____
_____
_____
_____
_____
_____
_____
_____
_____
_____
_____
_____
_____
_____
_____
_____
_____
_____
_____
_____
_____
_____
_____
_____

Copyright © 2019. Virlynn Smith Randolph. All rights reserved.

The Courage to BLOOM Journal & Guide

Day 22

Today is a day of unlimited opportunity. I must only CHOOSE to make things happen.

Success is not just for SOME of us. It is for ALL of us. Once you know that your success is unlimited, then you will continue to make choices that move you into the success realm.

What are you choosing to make happen today?

Copyright © 2019. Virlynn Smith Randolph. All rights reserved.

The Courage to BLOOM Journal & Guide 🌹

Daily Reflections of a Rose

_____
_____
_____
_____
_____
_____
_____
_____
_____
_____
_____
_____
_____
_____
_____
_____
_____
_____
_____
_____
_____
_____
_____
_____

Copyright © 2019. Virlynn Smith Randolph. All rights reserved.

The Courage to BLOOM Journal & Guide 🌹

Day 23

I live the life that I choose by my actions. Today I choose ONLY those things that will bless my future.

Your choices have gotten you where you are. If you don't like where you are, have the courage to make some new choices. Take responsibility for where past choices have led you and use your mind to move to a different place.

Copyright © 2019. Virlynn Smith Randolph. All rights reserved.

The Courage to BLOOM Journal & Guide

Daily Reflections of a Rose

_____
_____
_____
_____
_____
_____
_____
_____
_____
_____
_____
_____
_____
_____
_____
_____
_____
_____
_____
_____
_____
_____
_____
_____
_____
_____
_____
_____

Copyright © 2019. Virlynn Smith Randolph. All rights reserved.

The Courage to BLOOM Journal & Guide 🌹

Day 24

I hold my head high and put a smile on my face daily.

There is something amazing that happens when you hold your head up and smile. It is the ultimate sign of confidence. Do you know that people are attracted to those who possess confidence? So even if you don't feel it 100% right now, then know that the more you hold your head high and smile, the more people will be attracted to you.

Copyright © 2019. Virlynn Smith Randolph. All rights reserved.

The Courage to BLOOM Journal & Guide 🌹

Daily Reflections of a Rose

_____
_____
_____
_____
_____
_____
_____
_____
_____
_____
_____
_____
_____
_____
_____
_____
_____
_____
_____
_____
_____
_____
_____
_____
_____
_____
_____
_____
_____

Copyright © 2019. Virlynn Smith Randolph. All rights reserved.

The Courage to BLOOM Journal & Guide 🌹

Day 25

The ONLY person I need to prove anything to is myself.

Your greatness and purpose were given to you by God at birth. The only person you need prove anything to is your creator. Stop letting people have power to make you "prove" to them what God has already said you were capable.

The Courage to BLOOM Journal & Guide 🌹

Daily Reflections of a Rose

_____
_____
_____
_____
_____
_____
_____
_____
_____
_____
_____
_____
_____
_____
_____
_____
_____
_____
_____
_____
_____
_____

Copyright © 2019. Virlynn Smith Randolph. All rights reserved.

The Courage to BLOOM Journal & Guide 🌹

Day 26

Because of my confidence I GIVE and RECEIVE compliments from others easily.

I am guilty of turning down compliments as well. Today, be deliberate about complimenting others and accepting the compliments that they give you. You deserve them.

The Courage to BLOOM Journal & Guide 🌹

Daily Reflections of a Rose

_____
_____
_____
_____
_____
_____
_____
_____
_____
_____
_____
_____
_____
_____
_____
_____
_____
_____
_____
_____
_____
_____
_____
_____
_____

Copyright © 2019. Virlynn Smith Randolph. All rights reserved.

The Courage to BLOOM Journal & Guide 🌹

Day 27

I think ONLY caring, positive and loving thoughts.

Take control of your mind. Spend more time in positive thoughts than you do with other thoughts. Remember your mouth controls your mind, so make sure you are repeating your affirmations throughout the day and setting the course for positive things to grow in your mind and in your life.

Copyright © 2019. Virlynn Smith Randolph. All rights reserved.

The Courage to BLOOM Journal & Guide 🌹

Daily Reflections of a Rose

_____
_____
_____
_____
_____
_____
_____
_____
_____
_____
_____
_____
_____
_____
_____
_____
_____
_____
_____
_____
_____
_____
_____
_____
_____
_____

Copyright © 2019. Virlynn Smith Randolph. All rights reserved.

The Courage to BLOOM Journal & Guide 🌹

Day 28

Today I am MY best me. I can't compare myself to others but I CAN be my best self always.

Being the real you can make your happy. Anytime you work to be your best self, you win. After all, who can be BETTER at being YOU than you!

Copyright © 2019. Virlynn Smith Randolph. All rights reserved.

The Courage to BLOOM Journal & Guide

Daily Reflections of a Rose

_____
_____
_____
_____
_____
_____
_____
_____
_____
_____
_____
_____
_____
_____
_____
_____
_____
_____
_____
_____
_____
_____
_____
_____

Copyright © 2019. Virlynn Smith Randolph. All rights reserved.

The Courage to BLOOM Journal & Guide

Day 29

I have the power to say "no" to any situation that doesn't make me happy or serve my future.

Boundaries are important on this journey. Make sure that you are not so busy saying 'yes' to others that you say 'no' to yourself. We are all on a journey to our next level. What makes someone else's journey more important than your own? The answer is nothing.

Copyright © 2019. Virlynn Smith Randolph. All rights reserved.

The Courage to BLOOM Journal & Guide

Daily Reflections of a Rose

_____
_____
_____
_____
_____
_____
_____
_____
_____
_____
_____
_____
_____
_____
_____
_____
_____
_____
_____
_____
_____
_____
_____
_____
_____
_____
_____
_____

Copyright © 2019. Virlynn Smith Randolph. All rights reserved.

The Courage to BLOOM Journal & Guide

Day 30

I know I have what it takes to be successful and I will NOT stop trying until I am happy with my life.

Success and happiness are both a process. WE can choose to continue moving towards both or give up at anytime. Choose progress. Choose happiness. Choose Success. Choose to Bloom.

Copyright © 2019. Virlynn Smith Randolph. All rights reserved.

The Courage to BLOOM Journal & Guide

Daily Reflections of a Rose

_____
_____
_____
_____
_____
_____
_____
_____
_____
_____
_____
_____
_____
_____
_____
_____
_____
_____
_____
_____
_____
_____
_____
_____
_____
_____
_____
_____
_____

Copyright © 2019. Virlynn Smith Randolph. All rights reserved.

Final Note from the Author

Continue to Bloom...

There was once a time when I didn't have the courage to bloom. There were just too many thorns. The ground was just too rocky. And to be honest, I just didn't know HOW to bloom.

I didn't know I had the permission to bloom.

Now I know that we are ALL **ROSES**. But sometimes we need someone to give us the permission to be our best. To live life in full bloom. To have the audacity to be great.

In order for you to CONTINUE TO BLOOM:

1. Complete your own list of personal affirmations. Address the areas where you feel you still need continued courage and confidence. Remember to phrase them

The Courage to BLOOM Journal & Guide

positive... there is no room for negative here.

2. Complete your bloom certificate below. Feel free to print it out and hang it on your wall as a reminder to the 30 days we spent together.

3. Consider continuing to read and journal something positive EACH day. Confidence and courage are a habit. If you don't feed them, then you leave room for "other" things we don't need to return.

4. Surround yourself ONLY with those things that help you grow as a **ROSE**. Remove all weeds, thorns, and bad soil. (People, places and things) that don't allow you to live LIFE in FULL Bloom!

Copyright © 2019. Virlynn Smith Randolph. All rights reserved.

[INSTRUCTIONS: Tear out certificate and share it on social media... be sure to use our community hashtag: #couragetobloom]

✂ -

~Your Bloom Commitment~

Today, I, Virlynn Smith Randolph, give you _____ the permission to live life in full bloom. I give you the courage to challenge those who think YOU are not a **ROSE**. I give you the right to ignore those who feel that you can't bloom.

And more importantly, I extend to you the LOVE to know that you CAN and SHOULD have the audacity to live life in full bloom.

Signed by: _____

Date: _____

Copyright © 2019. Virlynn Smith Randolph. All rights reserved.

My Personal Affirmations 🌹

_____
_____
_____
_____
_____
_____
_____
_____
_____
_____
_____
_____

My Personal Affirmations 🌹

_____
_____
_____
_____
_____
_____
_____

Copyright © 2019. Virlynn Smith Randolph. All rights reserved.

My Personal Affirmations 🌹

My Personal Affirmations 🌹

_____
_____
_____
_____
_____
_____
_____
_____
_____
_____
_____
_____

My Personal Affirmations 🌹

_____
_____
_____
_____
_____
_____

Copyright © 2019. Virlynn Smith Randolph. All rights reserved.

My Personal Affirmations 🌹

About the Author

Virlynn Smith Randolph is known for supporting, encouraging, and inspiring women to help them regain their power, courage and self-esteem; she helps them to remove the thorns of life that have accumulated through pain, hurt and rejection, so that they may

Copyright © 2019. Virlynn Smith Randolph. All rights reserved.

emerge into full bloom, from Adversity to Audacity.

Virlynn is best known for her ability to help others overcome their circumstances and rebuild with inner strength through prayer and determination. She is also known for her ability to connect with others and help them to see the best of themselves, even when the world has told them the worst.

As a retired station manager of the Washington Metropolitan Area Transit Authority, Virlynn transitioned her 30 years of award-winning customer service skills into stellar responsiveness for her clients.

As Station Manager, she received numerous awards and recognition in excellence for her customer service. This passion for customer service spills over into the multiple events she has coordinated for her church, community, and clients.

Virlynn serves as a Co-Host to the wildly popular, Build Your Online Business Morning Show, and has spoken for numerous women's conference, both virtual and in-person across the country.

Friends describe her as loving, kind, dependable, trustworthy, driven, funny and no nonsense. She is well-known for her personality, her ability to convey emotion with conversation, and her ability to get along well with others.

As a mother of two grown daughters, Virlynn is known to be an advocate for the less fortunate and disadvantaged.

Copyright © 2019. Virlynn Smith Randolph. All rights reserved.

Rose of Audacity: The Audacity to Bloom was written to help women remove the thorns that LIFE has given them and create their BEST life from what God has given them. After blooming herself, Virlynn is now ready to spread her wings, sharing confident messages to the world.

~ THANKS FOR YOUR SUPPORT! ~

Copyright © 2019. Virlynn Smith Randolph. All rights reserved.

www.ingramcontent.com/pod-product-compliance
Lightning Source LLC
Chambersburg PA
CBHW051704090426
42736CB00013B/2531